Who Was
Milton Hershey?

Who Was
Milton Hershey?

By James Buckley Jr.

Illustrated by Ted Hammond

Grosset & Dunlap

An Imprint of Penguin Group (USA) LLC

For Patty, who loves chocolate—JB

To Mom—TH

GROSSET & DUNLAP
Published by the Penguin Group
Penguin Group (USA) LLC, 375 Hudson Street, New York, New York 10014, USA

USA | Canada | UK | Ireland | Australia | New Zealand | India | South Africa | China

penguin.com
A Penguin Random House Company

Library of Congress Control Number: 2013032705

ISBN 978-0-448-47936-1   10 9 8

Contents

Who Was
Milton Hershey?

An American candy store in 1900 looked very different than it does today. Candy was a special treat sold almost exclusively in candy stores. Customers didn't touch the merchandise, and it certainly wasn't available in wrappers and bars. It was not displayed on open racks, but held in glass jars behind a counter. Shop clerks put candy into

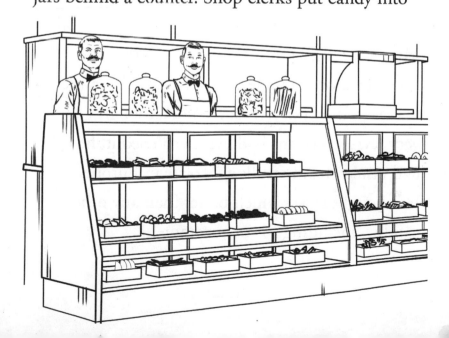

bags, one small piece at a time. The many varieties of candy included butterscotch, toffee, caramel, molasses candy, taffy, and hard candy made from boiled sugar in dozens of flavors and colors.

Even though there was plenty to choose from, Milton Hershey knew the one thing that was missing: chocolate. He was a successful caramel maker from Pennsylvania. And, although very few Americans had ever even tried it, he had tasted creamy milk chocolate in Europe. He thought it was much better than any other candy—including his own caramels!

Hershey put all his energy and time into bringing milk chocolate to America. After many years of experimenting, he succeeded beyond his wildest dreams. The Hershey chocolate bar changed the way Americans bought and enjoyed candy. It was affordable, portable, and individually wrapped. The bar was sold in drugstores and grocery stores and, best of all, made chocolate available to everyone.

Milton Hershey's success helped him realize other dreams, too—creating towns, improving manufacturing methods, helping children, and leaving a rich, chocolate legacy millions still enjoy today.

Chapter 1
Time to Get to Work

If you love chocolate, then you should celebrate every September 13. On that day in 1857, Milton Snavely Hershey was born in a house in Hockersville, Pennsylvania. It was a town in the lovely Lebanon Valley. Milton would later become world famous for making chocolate, but he spent almost all his life not far from the house in which he was born.

Milton's parents were Henry and Fanny Hershey. Henry was a dreamer. He loved reading

HENRY HERSHEY

and trying new things.
Henry was always looking
for the next big idea,
even if he didn't know
what it was.

FANNY HERSHEY

By 1860, Henry's
farm had failed.
Henry moved his
small family to
Titusville, Pennsylvania.
Oil had been discovered
there, and he wanted to make his fortune by
pumping oil. Henry also tried selling supplies to
the prospectors pouring into the area. Neither
idea worked. Within a year and a half, Fanny's
family had to pay to bring the Hershey family
back home.

They tried farming again. Milton loved it,
feeding the chickens and picking berries. To
help out, he sometimes sold the berries to their

neighbors. His family didn't have much money,
so every bit helped. Milton was always careful
with whatever money he got. In 1863, a Civil War

battle was fought at nearby Gettysburg. Milton took his coins and buried them in a can in the garden for safekeeping. Then later, he couldn't find the can!

Along with his new baby sister, Sarena, Milton and his parents moved again later in 1863. Fanny's family helped the Hersheys buy a farm called Nine Points. In this new place, Milton was sent to yet another new school. He was not a good student and didn't like school that much. He had already been in several by the time he was nine.

At Nine Points, Henry Hershey tried farming again . . . and failed again. Though Fanny sold eggs and Milton helped out, life was hard for the Hersheys.

In 1867, Sarena, Milton's sister, became very ill. She was just shy of her fifth birthday when she died of scarlet fever. That was the final straw for Fanny. Though she didn't directly blame Henry, she turned her back on him. They could not get a divorce. Her religion didn't allow it. They did split up, however, which was very unusual in those days. Milton stayed with his mother.

In 1870, Milton's school days ended. He was twelve, but he could only read and write as well as a fourth grader. Fanny had no problem with that. She said that it was time for Milton to get a real job.

Chapter 2
The Young Candy Maker

Milton's first job did not work out. He was working for a printer. It was difficult and boring. One day, he took matters into his own hands. He let his straw hat drop into one of the printing machines while it was running. The machine stopped working . . . and a few minutes later, so did Milton.

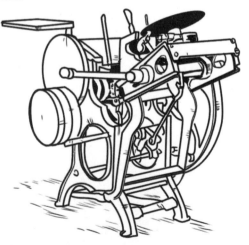

ROYER'S
Ice Cream Garden

Fanny suggested that a job at an ice cream parlor would be more fun. So Milton started working at Royer's Ice Cream Parlor and Garden in Lancaster, Pennsylvania. It was *much* more fun than printing. Lancaster was a bigger city, too, with many more people and things to see.

Milton had learned from his mother how to work hard. So he put in long hours mixing, stirring, wrapping, and selling Royer's products, such as ice cream, juices, and candy. From his father, however, Milton got a love of trying new things. At Royer's he saw how the owner mixed different kinds of ingredients together to try new candies. Milton wanted to make his own candies.

So he started experimenting with his own ideas.
Royer's was located in a busy part of the city.
College students came in to buy ice cream and
sweets. Businessmen came by during lunch.

Milton often kept an eye on the horses of customers while they shopped. One customer liked Milton so much that he always tossed the boy a dime in thanks.

After Milton had worked at Royer's for four years, Fanny encouraged him to move onward and upward. She hoped that her son would be more than just a shop assistant. In 1876, Milton took his first big step into business. Although only nineteen, Milton opened his own candy shop in Philadelphia, about seventy-five miles away. The big city was booming. It was 1876, America was celebrating its one hundredth birthday, and thousands of people were joining the party. Hershey borrowed money from his aunt Mattie. Milton's shop on Spring Garden Street was a hit from the start. He really knew how to bring

people in. He ran a pipe up from the basement, where he cooked the candy, to the ground floor. People smelled the boiling sugar and came to satisfy their sweet tooth.

Hershey's shop sold candy that he made himself, along with fruit and ice cream. He didn't sell chocolate, however. At that time, chocolate was a luxury item. It was very expensive to make. It also melted very quickly, and couldn't be sold in warm weather. In fact, many people in America had never tasted chocolate. For the moment, the name Hershey meant taffy and sugar candy.

Sales were good at first. Milton could make great candy, but he was not a great businessman. The store did not make a profit. Perhaps more

schooling might have helped Milton, but it was
too late for that. He worked so hard that early in
1881, he got sick. He had to spend a month in bed
getting better.

In early 1882, Milton Hershey had to close
his candy shop. Wagons from Lancaster arrived
in Philadelphia. Milton's cousins were on board.
They filled the wagons with gear and kettles from
the shop. Hershey turned his back on Philadelphia
and headed home.

To his mother's surprise, Milton's next move was to follow his father. Henry had written to say that he was in Colorado mining for gold, and that Milton should join him. It was a move that would change all their lives.

Milton arrived in Colorado as the gold was running out. Once again, Henry had missed his dream. But Milton stayed and tried to make the best of it. He got a job at a candy company. The store sold a sweet treat called caramel. Milton

had seen caramel before, but never like this! It was soft and creamy and didn't get stale on the shelf. He learned that the secret was to mix in fresh milk, not the wax that other caramel makers used.

Milton memorized everything about making the perfect caramel. Then he decided to open his own shop again. By 1883, he had traveled back across the country to New York, the biggest city in the United States. At first he worked at a fancy shop called Huyler's. In his free time he explored the city, looking for a place to open his own shop.

In this period, New York City's candy shops sold to their own neighborhoods. If you wanted candy, you went to your local store. Candy was not sold in nearly as many places as it is today. So Milton needed a neighborhood without a candy store.

He decided that Sixth Avenue near Forty-Second Street was the right place. Today, surrounded by skyscrapers, it is one of the busiest corners in the city. In 1884, it was not nearly so busy. There was a park across the street and

small buildings. But Milton's shop did pretty
well for a while. People going to a nearby theater
often stopped in. A new hotel brought in more
customers. Fanny and Aunt Mattie once again
came to help, mostly with wrapping the treats
Milton cooked up in the basement.

When people came into his store, Milton helped them choose candy. In those days, candy store clerks helped with every purchase. There were no counters filled with pre-wrapped candy. Instead, candy was kept in glass cases or glass jars behind the counter. Often customers could buy several pieces of candy for just a penny. They would point to their favorites and the clerks would count them out and carefully wrap them in paper.

Unfortunately, Milton had to close the store in 1886. His father, Henry, was partly to blame. The year before, Henry had arrived in New York City and wanted his son to try making cough drops. But the special machines needed to form the drops were very expensive and the cough-drop adventure ended up costing Milton his business. The store was ruined, and Milton headed home to Pennsylvania. But Milton still had something valuable. He still knew how to make amazing caramels. He was not ready to give up the candy business.

Chapter 3
Success!

Along with his secret caramel recipe, Milton had learned something else in his travels. Selling caramels one at a time was nice, but selling them in big batches was better. With one sale to a hotel or restaurant, he could make as much as selling to several dozen individual customers.

He borrowed money from a bank to start a
small caramel factory in Lancaster. Milton was
soon selling his tasty caramels. Then something
amazing happened. Milton got the big break
he had been waiting for. A man from England
was visiting Lancaster. He tried one of Milton's
caramels and loved it. He placed a huge order that
had to be delivered to England in three months.
With such a big order, Milton paid off a bank
loan and bought more equipment and ingredients.

So Hershey's factory made the order and sent the caramels across the Atlantic Ocean.

Milton Hershey was finally a success!

The Lancaster Caramel Company boomed. Milton kept experimenting. The caramel got even better. He called it Crystal A Caramel. He sold huge amounts to stores, restaurants, delis, and more.

Having his factory in Lancaster taught Hershey a few things about location. First, cows on Lancaster farms provided all the milk that he needed to make caramel. Also, Lancaster itself was near one of the new electric plants, so his factory's machines had plenty of power. Railroads connected his factory to the places where the sugar and flavorings came from to make the candy and to the cities where the candy orders were sent. He also relied on the hardworking people who lived in the area. Lancaster was a great place for his caramel company.

And Milton Hershey loved making candy. Milton spent hours trying new ways to make caramels. He tried putting nuts in some brands.

He tried icing. He even made some caramels that were less expensive, so more folks could afford them. Milton didn't just play the role of boss, either. He rolled up his sleeves and mixed caramel in the huge vats, too. He wanted to make sure his caramels were the best they could be.

By the early 1890s, the company had two factories and more than thirteen hundred workers. Thanks to caramel—and hard work—Milton Hershey was soon one of richest men in Lancaster. He bought a big house for himself and another one for his mother. He also made his first trips to Europe. While in England, he saw that some candy companies were starting to sell chocolate. They were inventing new ways to make chocolate so that it could be easily stored and sold. That got Milton thinking.

Chapter 4
Mr. Hershey Goes to Chicago

In 1893, another trip changed Milton's life.
That year, he went to Chicago for the World's
Columbian Exposition. It was held to celebrate the

four hundred years since Christopher Columbus had arrived in the New World.

For the fair, dozens of new buildings were put up in a Chicago park. All were made from wood and white stucco. The fair was nicknamed the "White City." There were exhibits from around the world. People could ride in boats on man-made lakes. They tasted new treats, including something called a "hamburger." Visitors rode the world's first Ferris wheel.

In one building with food exhibits, Milton saw something that made him stop in his tracks. A German candy company had made a temple out of chocolate. It stood thirty-eight feet tall—about as tall as a four-story building. Hershey was stunned. And in a building with machinery exhibits there were iron machines, clanking and puffing away.

The machines were making chocolate.

The J.M. Lehmann Company from Germany had set up a complete chocolate-making factory right there in the White City. A machine roasted the raw cacao beans. Another machine ground the roasted beans into powder. Into the powder went sugar and flavorings. Hershey watched the machine for hours. He asked endless questions. He returned again and again, even bringing friends and people from his company to see the machine.

THE HISTORY OF CHOCOLATE

CHOCOLATE IS MADE FROM THE CACAO (KUH-COW) PLANT. CACAO GROWS ON TREES IN PLACES WHERE IT IS HOT AND HUMID. SCIENTISTS CALL THE PLANT *THEOBROMA CACAO*, WHICH MEANS "FOOD OF THE GODS." PODS ABOUT THE SIZE OF FOOTBALLS GROW ON THE TREE. INSIDE EACH POD ARE ABOUT THIRTY TO FORTY CACAO BEANS THAT ARE THE SIZE OF STRAWBERRIES. IT TAKES ABOUT THREE HUNDRED AND FIFTY BEANS TO MAKE ONE POUND OF CHOCOLATE.

THE ANCIENT AZTECS AND MAYA HARVESTED CACAO PODS FROM TREES IN CENTRAL AMERICA. THEY MIXED THE GROUND-UP BEANS WITH WATER TO MAKE A BITTER

BUT POPULAR DRINK. THE WORD *CHOCOLATE* COMES FROM *XOCOATL*, THE AZTEC WORD FOR THIS DRINK.

IN THE 1500S, INVADING SPANISH SOLDIERS DRANK IT AND DISLIKED IT. WHEN IT WAS TRIED IN SPAIN, THE SPANISH ADDED SUGAR OR HONEY. SWEET CHOCOLATE WAS BORN. THEN, IN 1847, AN ENGLISH COMPANY, J.S. FRY & SONS, FOUND A WAY TO MIX CACAO BUTTER WITH CACAO POWDER. WHEN IT HARDENED, IT WAS A CHOCOLATE BAR. FINALLY, IN 1875, SWISS SCIENTISTS DANIEL PETER AND HENRI NESTLÉ MIXED MILK WITH CHOCOLATE TO MAKE IT EVEN CREAMIER.

HENRI NESTLÉ

TODAY, SEVERAL COUNTRIES IN AFRICA PRODUCE MOST OF THE WORLD'S CACAO USED TO MAKE CHOCOLATE. THE NUMBER-ONE CACAO-PRODUCING COUNTRY IS CÔTE D'IVOIRE, ON THE WEST COAST OF AFRICA. CACAO ALSO GROWS IN GHANA, INDONESIA, AND IN SOUTH AMERICA.

His cousin, Frank Snavely, said that Milton told him, "The caramel business is a fad. But chocolate is something we will always have."

Hershey was so convinced of this that he bought every piece of gear that Lehmann had in Chicago. He even ordered more machines from Germany. He took everything back to Lancaster where Milton set up the new Hershey Chocolate Company in a corner of his caramel factory.

As he had with caramels, Milton experimented. The chocolate made by the new German machines was good, but it wasn't perfect. It was still a little bit bitter. Milton wanted to make milk chocolate, as Nestlé had done. Milk chocolate was sweeter and lasted longer than the chocolate available at the time. It could be molded into shapes. It would not melt as quickly as regular chocolate.

One big problem: Nestlé wouldn't share the secret.

Milton returned to his family's first home,
which he used as a lab to work out a new chocolate
formula. He mixed and poured and sampled and
cooked. He tried and tried again . . . and finally he

got pretty close. Hershey came up with a recipe for a type of milk chocolate. With that recipe in hand, he made a big decision. Milton Hershey decided to sell his caramel company and devote all his energy to chocolate. It was a huge risk. But Hershey was confident that chocolate was the future!

Chapter 5
Here Comes Kitty

Milton Hershey didn't spend all his time working. In 1897, he met Catherine Sweeney, who was nicknamed Kitty, at a candy shop in upstate New York, where he had traveled to sell caramel. She and Milton began seeing a lot of each other. She later moved to New York City, and he visited her there often. Hershey didn't tell anyone back home about Kitty until after they were married in May 1898. His family and the candy company workers were very surprised when he first brought her home. Hershey was forty-one at the time, a successful and serious businessman. Kitty was only twenty-six and enjoyed shopping, entertaining, and having fun. Together, they would make a terrific team.

In 1900, with his chocolate dreams in mind, Hershey sold the Lancaster Caramel Company for $1 million. A new century was starting, and

America was about to get its first candy bar.

After the sale Milton took Kitty to Europe. They visited many countries in Europe, including France, Germany, and Austria. They also traveled to Egypt, where they rode camels near the famous pyramids. Milton also made sure to try many types of candy. He was always looking for new ideas for his company.

Milton loved spending time with Kitty away from the factory. With her, he could relax and not be the boss. Milton liked to gamble and play cards. Unlike other very wealthy businessmen, he didn't spend much money on himself. But he loved to buy Kitty jewels and furs.

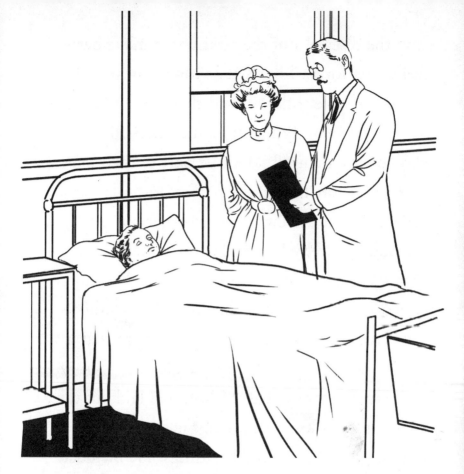

Sadly, he also had to spend money on many
doctors. Though Kitty seemed healthy, she had a
disease that often weakened her muscles. Milton
did his best to help her. He took her to doctor
after doctor trying to find a cure. No one could

stop the disease. But they did try to make her feel better for a while. Kitty's illness meant she could not have children, and that was a terrible disappointment. But Milton and Kitty found a way to have many children be part of their lives.

Even before he had the perfect formula for milk chocolate, Milton took another big risk. He bought twelve hundred acres in nearby Derry Church. Hershey wanted to build a huge chocolate factory and a town for all its workers. He planned everything from the start so that it would all be perfect. Before the Hershey factory made one chocolate bar, Milton had laid out the streets and parks of his town. He hired architects to design the homes and buildings. He included a bank, a zoo, and schools. Hershey even set up a trolley-car line to help workers get around town and travel to and from the factory.

Then he built the huge factory. Its giant smokestacks had his name in big letters. Hershey

tried something else new: He made chocolate on an assembly line. An assembly line is a way to make a product by adding one thing at a time as the product moves along a work line. Instead

of one worker making a product by himself, the steps are divided up among many workers. Each is in charge of one step, which the worker does over and over. Products can be made faster and in

greater numbers this way. In Detroit, Henry Ford
had used the assembly line to make cars.

The plant soon sent the smell of chocolate
floating all over the valley. As the workers moved
into the town, they enjoyed the smell, too.
Though the town did not have an official name
yet, people were already calling it "the sweetest
place on Earth."

While his dream town and factory grew, Hershey kept experimenting with chocolate. Finally, by early 1904, he was satisfied. He had a way to make milk chocolate that could be shipped safely. It was sweet, creamy, and could be molded into bars. It would last for several days without being kept cold. All of America—not just Pennsylvania—was about to get its first real taste of milk chocolate.

Each bar was wrapped in dark maroon paper with large gold letters that said HERSHEY. Each bar cost just five cents. By 1905, the factory was making as much as a hundred thousand pounds of chocolate a day.

CHOCOLATE THE HERSHEY WAY

AFTER THE CACAO BEANS WERE PICKED, CLEANED, AND DRIED, THEY WERE ROASTED. A SPECIAL MACHINE ROLLED THE BEANS TO TAKE OFF THE HARD OUTER SHELLS. THEN THE BEANS WERE GROUND INTO A LIQUID CALLED COCOA LIQUOR. THE LIQUID WAS MIXED WITH SUGAR, VANILLA, MILK, AND ANY FLAVORS NEEDED. HUGE MACHINES MIXED AND STIRRED ALL THE INGREDIENTS TOGETHER IN A SECRET PROCESS. THIS RESULTED IN A COARSE POWDER CALLED CHOCOLATE CRUMB. COCOA BUTTER WAS ADDED, AND THEN THE CHOCOLATE WAS MIXED AGAIN.

AFTER THE MIXTURE WAS RIGHT, MACHINES POURED THE LIQUID CHOCOLATE INTO MOLDS. THE MOLDS PUT HERSHEY'S NAME ON EACH BAR. AFTER THE CHOCOLATE COOLED, A WORKER KNOCKED THE BARS OUT OF THE MOLD WITH A HAMMER. THEN THE BARS WERE WRAPPED IN PAPER AND PUT IN BOXES.

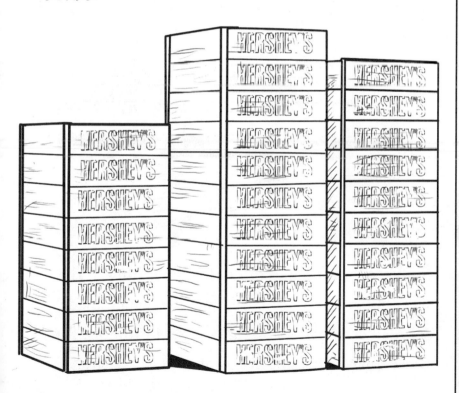

Chapter 6
Chocolate Town, USA

Milton Hershey made great chocolate. But he also made a great town. The idea of building a whole town for a company's workers was not new.

Some coal mines had done the same thing in the late 1800s. The Pullman Company, which made railroad cars, had a company town in Illinois. But those towns were not nearly as nice as Hershey,

Pennsylvania. In other company towns, the houses were not very well made. The workers had to buy all their food at the company store, too, where prices were often high. There was nothing to do for fun in those towns, either.

In Hershey's town, he included parks and theaters. Hershey houses were comfortable and attractive. They had electricity and indoor plumbing. At the time, many American homes still did not have flush toilets!

As the years went on, Hershey kept adding to the town. In 1904, he built a library and a post office. In 1905, he built a bank so that workers could save their money. Also in 1905 a zoo was added. (The Hershey Park Zoo caused some problems. The monkeys were very good at escaping. But townspeople just called the zoo when they saw them scampering on their lawns. Another time, a worker found little monkey footprints in the chocolate factory!)

In 1907, he opened a huge park for all residents. In 1910, he opened a general store so

that they could shop close to home. Over the years, he gave money to different religious groups so they could build churches in the town, too.

Milton chose all the street names in his town. Many had something to do with chocolate. You might live on streets named for Java or Ceylon, places where cacao beans were grown. Areba Avenue was named for a type of cacao bean. The town's main intersection was Chocolate Avenue and Cocoa Avenue.

Hershey was different from many very rich men of this time. He felt very strongly that anyone who had plenty of money ought to share it. Though he never followed a particular religion, he said he followed the Golden Rule. He wanted to do for other people what he hoped they would do for him. His workers made the chocolate that made him rich. So he wanted to make sure they shared in the success. In fact, he gave them a bonus each year from the company's profits.

Hershey brought chocolate to America. But his idea of how a business owner should conduct himself was probably more important.

The town really needed a name. In 1904, the US Post Office said it needed to know where mail should be sent. A contest was held to pick

a name. Among the finalists were Beansdale, Majestic, St. Milton's, and Zenith. The winner was Hersheykoko, but the post office turned that one down. It sounded like a product, not a town! Finally, the choice was obvious. In 1906, the new town was officially named Hershey, Pennsylvania.

Chapter 7
Spreading the Wealth

A few years after opening, the Hershey factory sold more than five million dollars worth of bars every year! (Today, that would be about 123 million dollars.) Milton didn't think he needed to branch out to different chocolate products. He was happy making chocolate in the classic chocolate-bar shape. But in 1907, he created one new product that would become even more famous than the Hershey chocolate bar.

Hershey's had a machine that dropped small amounts of chocolate on a conveyor belt. The candies were first called Sweethearts. The story goes that when each drop hit the conveyor belt, it made was a small smacking sound. Milton heard the sound and came up with a new, better name.

The Hershey's Kiss was born. Soon millions of the Kisses were being hand-wrapped in the factory. Workers put a small tissue label on the candy. Then they spun it all inside a small piece of foil. Until 1921, every Kiss was wrapped by hand. Hershey's mother, Fanny, who lived in a big house near the factory, still wanted to help. She had a box of unwrapped Kisses sent to her every day. She wrapped them and gave them to visitors. (Visitors to Hershey, Pennsylvania, today can see

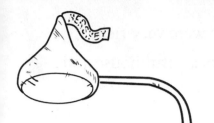

that some of the town's streetlights are in the shape of Kisses.)

It was important to Milton that his chocolate was affordable. He wanted everyone to enjoy chocolate. For sixty years, until 1969, Hershey bars cost only five cents. And you could find them everywhere. It used to be that a candy store was the only place to buy candy. But Milton told his salesmen to go everywhere: drugstores, grocery stores, lunch counters, gift stores—anywhere people might want to buy chocolate bars.

Milton and Kitty Hershey were very rich.
They had built themselves a beautiful house and

gardens on a hill overlooking the factory. They were beloved by the people of the town, for whom they had done so much.

The couple always missed not having children of their own. So the Hersheys came up with a way to care for and raise many kids. In 1909, Milton started the Hershey Industrial School for orphan boys.

In the early 1900s, there was great concern over what to do for orphan boys. There were orphan girls, too, of course. But in those days, girls could get jobs that didn't require much training. They became cooks or seamstresses or housekeepers. Boys, it was thought, needed more schooling to prepare them for jobs in factories or in stores. The difference in the way boys and girls were treated was not fair. But that's how it was.

Hershey's school was meant to give orphan boys the skills needed to earn a decent living. The school also gave them a home.

Hershey himself had bounced from school to school. He wanted to make sure other boys avoided that. At the school, boys lived in family

homes with foster parents. Other schools for orphan boys had big dorms where everyone slept in one room. Hershey didn't want that; he wanted the boys to feel comfortable and loved.

The school accepted orphans from nearby counties. Some poor families that had several kids could also send their boys to the school to live and study. All the boys studied reading and basic math.

They learned trades such as carpentry and
farming. They also worked on the school's farm,
milking cows every morning.

Because Milton Hershey also believed in having fun, Hershey Park grew and grew. He added a carousel, bowling alleys, and a miniature railroad. There were concerts and shows and, in the winter, ice skating. Most of these things were

free to the citizens of Hershey, Pennsylvania.
Thousands of visitors came, too. By the end of
1913, more than a hundred thousand people had
visited Hershey Park.

As all these things were going on in the town

THE PARK TODAY

BY THE 1950S, MILTON HERSHEY'S LOVELY GREEN PARK FOR HIS EMPLOYEES HAD BLOSSOMED INTO A HUGE AMUSEMENT PARK. BY THE 1960S, HOWEVER, IT WAS ALL A BIT RUN-DOWN. IN 1971, THE HERSHEY ENTERTAINMENT COMPANY MADE A BIG CHANGE. THEY PUT A FENCE AROUND IT AND STARTED CHARGING AN ENTRANCE FEE. MANY PEOPLE WERE UPSET AT THE TIME. EVENTUALLY, THOUGH, THE NEW HERSHEYPARK WOULD BECOME A VERY POPULAR PLACE.

HERSHEYPARK TODAY BOASTS ELEVEN ROLLER COASTERS. SKYRUSH IS THE TALLEST AT MORE THAN

TWO HUNDRED FEET AND TAKES RIDERS AS FAST
AS SEVENTY-FIVE MILES PER HOUR. VISITORS
CAN CHOOSE FROM SEVERAL WATER SLIDES, TOO,
INCLUDING THE DIZZYING COASTLINE PLUNGE,
VORTEX, AND TIDAL FORCE, ONE OF THE TALLEST
WATER RIDES IN THE WORLD. HERSHEYPARK ALSO
HAS LOG RIDES, A MONORAIL, AN ENORMOUS
WAVE POOL, AND A ZOO.

LOCATED NOT FAR FROM THE HERSHEY FACTORY,
THE PARK ATTRACTS MORE THAN TWO MILLION
PEOPLE EACH YEAR.

of Hershey, Milton and Kitty continued to travel whenever her health allowed. In 1912, they made another trip to Europe. Milton had bought tickets on a famous ocean liner for their voyage home. However, because of a business meeting, he had to change plans and take an earlier ship. That

turned out to be an incredible stroke of luck for the Hersheys. The original ship they were to sail on was the *Titanic*, which was called the most luxurious ship ever made. The massive ocean liner hit an iceberg and sank on the way to America.

Luck was with them on that trip, but it ran out for Kitty not long after. She was visiting friends in Philadelphia when she became very ill. Milton rushed to her side. After years of poor health, Kitty died on March 25, 1915.

THE *TITANIC* TRAGEDY

   MILTON AND KITTY HERSHEY ESCAPED TRAGEDY
BY NOT SAILING ON THE RMS *TITANIC*. THE SHIP
WAS ON ITS FIRST TRIP ACROSS THE ATLANTIC
FROM ENGLAND TO AMERICA. AT THE TIME, THE
TITANIC WAS THE LARGEST SHIP EVER BUILT—
AND THE FANCIEST. FIRST-CLASS PASSENGERS
USED CHINA DISHES AND FANCY SILVERWARE. THEY
COULD SWIM IN A SMALL POOL OR PLAY SQUASH
ON A COURT. THERE WERE PLAYROOMS FOR

CHILDREN AND SHOWERS IN THE STATEROOMS. AN ORCHESTRA ENTERTAINED PASSENGERS. ONE BUILDER SAID THAT EVERYTHING ON BOARD WAS "THE FINEST MONEY COULD BUY."

THE *TITANIC* WAS SAID TO BE "PRACTICALLY UNSINKABLE." HOWEVER, ON APRIL 14, 1912, THE *TITANIC* STRUCK A HUGE ICEBERG AS IT NEARED CANADA AND SPLIT IN HALF BEFORE IT SUNK. THERE WERE NOT ENOUGH LIFEBOATS TO GET EVERYONE SAFELY OFF. SADLY, MORE THAN FIFTEEN HUNDRED PEOPLE DIED IN THE ICY WATERS BEFORE RESCUE COULD ARRIVE.

Milton never married again, and he kept pictures of Kitty in every room in his house for the rest of his life. Twice a week he had fresh flowers put on the grave of his beloved Kitty.

Chapter 8
Life after Kitty

Milton missed Kitty terribly. In her memory, he did something truly remarkable, and he did it in secret.

In 1918, not long after Kitty died, Milton gave all his stock in the Hershey Chocolate Company to the school. (Since 1951, it has been called the Milton Hershey School.) He also made the gift without telling anyone at his company. It was not until five years later that anyone outside the school knew about it. The news leaked when a newspaper revealed the gift.

Milton did this to make sure the school would keep going long after he was gone. Today, the

school still owns stock worth more than *nine billion dollars*! The Hershey School is richer than most universities in America. In fact, the school is so wealthy that in 1963 it could afford to build a hospital. The Penn State Hershey Medical Center is in Hershey, and is one of the biggest in the state.

The only rule Milton made about his gift was that it had to be used to help the students and the school. He watched over the school for the rest of his life. He treated the boys like his sons. He would often visit them in their homes with their foster parents. They also came to visit Milton at his house and have tea.

Once a year, he invited the whole school for a breakfast. Starting in 1930, the school has had a homecoming picnic for former students every year. For their part, the students loved Mr. Hershey.

Much of the sugar needed to make Hershey chocolate came from the island nation of Cuba. After Kitty's death, Milton visited and fell in love with the tropical country.

His mother, Fanny, had died in 1920, so Milton had less reason to stay in Hershey. So in the 1920s and 1930s, he spent as much as half his time in Cuba. He bought up several sugarcane farms. He built a factory to process the sugarcane into sugar for his chocolate. Then he built new houses for the workers on the farms. He also made sure the houses had electricity, which was very rare in Cuba at that time. He used the same generosity and creativity in Cuba that he had in Pennsylvania.

HERSHEY, CUBA

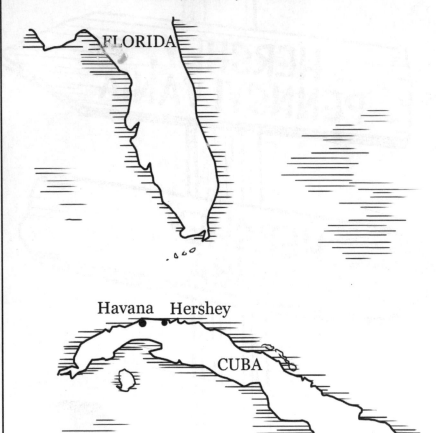

NINETY MILES OFF THE COAST OF FLORIDA,
HERSHEY, CUBA, WAS ONCE A THRIVING SUGAR-
PROCESSING CENTER. IT WAS HERE THAT
MILTON HERSHEY BUILT A BEAUTIFUL LITTLE TOWN

TO HOUSE AND SUPPORT THE EMPLOYEES OF HIS
SUGAR FACTORY AND SUGARCANE FIELDS. JUST
THIRTY-FIVE MILES FROM THE CAPITAL CITY OF
HAVANA, THE TOWN HAD SHOPS, A HOTEL, PARKS
AND GARDENS, AND ITS OWN TRAIN LINE. IT WAS
A LOT LIKE HERSHEY, PENNSYLVANIA. HOWEVER,
HERSHEY SOLD THE TOWN IN 1946, AND SADLY, IT
HAS NOT BEEN KEPT UP. ALTHOUGH MOST OF
HERSHEY, CUBA, IS NOW IN NEED OF RESTORATION,
ABOUT TWO HUNDRED FAMILIES LIVE THERE TODAY.

In the 1930s, America and the rest of the world went into an economic depression. Millions of people lost their jobs. Millions lost their homes. It was a terrible time for many in America. But it

was not so bad in Hershey, Pennsylvania.
Milton made sure that everyone in his factories
kept working. If they weren't making chocolate,
he found them jobs elsewhere. He put up

several new buildings in town. Then he built a
huge sports arena for an ice hockey team. The
deluxe Hotel Hershey was completed. A massive

new community building went up, too. Today, it is part of the company headquarters.

Since his chocolate bars were still only a nickel, people could afford to keep buying them. The factory stayed open and Hershey—the company and the town—survived the Depression.

HERSHEY'S GOES TO WAR

IN 1917, MILTON GOT A CHANCE TO HELP THE COUNTRY THAT HAD GIVEN HIM SO MUCH. WITH AMERICAN TROOPS HEADING OFF TO EUROPE TO FIGHT IN WORLD WAR I, HE TOLD THE GOVERNMENT HE WOULD PROVIDE CHOCOLATE BARS FOR SOLDIERS. THEY WOULD NEED ENERGY, HE SAID, TO DO THEIR WORK. MILLIONS OF BARS WERE IN THE RATION PACKS OF US SOLDIERS FROM 1917 TO 1918.

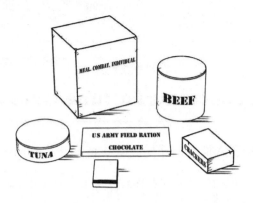

IN 1942, HERSHEY'S CREATED A SPECIAL
CHOCOLATE BAR CALLED A D-RATION THAT WOULD
NOT MELT EASILY. SOLDIERS FIGHTING WORLD
WAR II IN EUROPE PASSED OUT BARS TO KIDS
THEY MET. THEY ALSO TRADED THEM WITH LOCAL
PEOPLE. THE HERSHEY COMPANY GOT SEVERAL
AWARDS FROM THE US GOVERNMENT FOR ITS
WORK IN HELPING SOLDIERS.

Chapter 9
A Chocolate Fortune Lives On

In 1937, Milton Hershey turned eighty years old. The town of Hershey gave him a big birthday party. They sang him a song and had a huge

cake in the sports arena. For his part, Milton was slowing down. He let his managers take over running much of the company. By 1940, sales of Hershey products were forty-four million dollars, the highest they had ever been. In only four years, sales had almost doubled, to more than eighty million dollars annually.

Meanwhile, Milton still liked experimenting.

He tried making gum and chocolate pie. He tried making candy with raisins and molasses. He even tried baking new kinds of muffins. Making soap was one of his oddest experiments. He ended up making way too much, and it wasn't very good. He even tried to sell some himself from a shop in Atlantic City, New Jersey. He also tried to make ice cream less expensive by making it without

milk, and chocolate with flavors such as celery, turnip, or beets. Few of these ideas really worked.

In 1930, Milton gave his own house, called High Point, to the town. It became the clubhouse for the golf club. In 1941, he hired Ben Hogan to work at the golf course. Hogan would go on to become one of the greatest golfers in the world.

With more free time, Milton loved driving around Hershey. He visited the factory buildings

HOGAN AND HERSHEY

MILTON HERSHEY WAS THE BIGGEST NAME IN CHOCOLATE. BEN HOGAN WOULD BECOME THE BIGGEST NAME IN GOLF. WHEN HERSHEY HIRED HIM AS THE HERSHEY GOLF CLUB HEAD PRO, HE GAVE HOGAN TIME TO KEEP PLAYING IN TOURNAMENTS. HOGAN WORKED AT THE CLUB FOR TEN YEARS. IN THAT TIME, HE WON DOZENS OF EVENTS, INCLUDING SEVERAL OF THE SPORT'S MAJOR TOURNAMENTS. IN 1949, HE WAS IN A TERRIBLE CAR ACCIDENT. MANY THOUGHT HE COULD NEVER PLAY AGAIN. THE HERSHEY CLUB SUPPORTED HIM THROUGHOUT HIS RECOVERY, AND HE CAME BACK NOT ONLY TO PLAY BUT ALSO TO WIN THE US OPEN IN 1950. HOGAN'S FAME ALSO MADE THE HERSHEY COUNTRY CLUB FAMOUS. THE COURSE STILL PLAYS HOST TO TOP PRO EVENTS, SUCH AS THE 2011 PGA PROFESSIONAL NATIONAL CHAMPIONSHIP.

and the school. At the community building, he sometimes sat underneath a large painting of himself. He hid behind a newspaper to hear what people said about him!

In September 1945, he celebrated his eighty-eighth birthday. A few friends threw him a party at the old family home. It was where he had been born and where he later created his famous milk chocolate. A few days later, he started having trouble breathing. Milton Hershey died of pneumonia on October 13, 1945.

The Hershey Chocolate Company has continued, of course. In the decades since Milton's death, the company has added new candy such as Reese's Peanut Butter Cups and the NutRageous bar. The company also bought other candy brands such as Twizzlers licorice and Ice Breakers mints. It is truly a candy empire.

And this empire was created by one man: Milton Hershey.

TIMELINE OF
MILTON HERSHEY'S LIFE

1857 —— Milton Hershey is born in Pennsylvania

1870 —— Hershey stops going to school

1872 —— Hershey gets job with Royer's Candy in Lancaster,
Pennsylvania

1882 —— The Hershey store in Philadelphia closes, and he
moves to Colorado

1886 —— Hershey starts the Lancaster Caramel Company

1893 —— The World's Columbian Exposition opens in Chicago.
Hershey buys chocolate-making machines he sees there

1898 —— Hershey marries Catherine "Kitty" Sweeney

1900 —— The Lancaster Caramel Company is sold for $1 million

1903 —— Work begins on the town of Hershey, Pennsylvania,
and the Hershey chocolate factory there

1909 —— The Hershey Industrial School opens, serving orphan boys

1915 —— Kitty Hershey dies

1918 —— Hershey gives the bulk of the stock in the company
to the Hershey School

1933 —— In the midst of the Depression, the Hotel Hershey opens

1945 —— Hershey dies

TIMELINE OF THE WORLD

Civil War begins	1861
President Abraham Lincoln assassinated	1865
Alexander Graham Bell makes the first telephone call	1876
Thomas Edison perfects the electric lightbulb	1879
Coca-Cola goes on sale In 1928, the company that makes the soda begins buying most of its sugar from Hershey's farms	1886
The first Kodak camera brings photography to everyone	1888
Henry Ford's factory finishes the first Model T, making cars affordable for millions of people	1908
America enters World War I in Europe	1917
Charles Lindbergh becomes the first man to fly solo across the Atlantic Ocean	1927
The stock market crashes and the Great Depression begins	1929
World War II begins in Europe	1939
America enters World War II after Japan attacks Pearl Harbor in Hawaii	1941
World War II ends	1945

BIBLIOGRAPHY

Brenner, Joël Glenn. **The Emperors of Chocolate: Inside the Secret World of Hershey and Mars**. New York: Random House, 1999.

Burford, Betty. **Chocolate by Hershey**. New York: Millbrook Press, 1994.

D'Antonio, Michael. **Hershey: Milton S. Hershey's Extraordinary Life of Wealth, Empire, and Utopian Dreams**. New York: Simon & Schuster, 2006.

www.hersheyarchives.org
The website of the Hershey Community Archives, a historical database dedicated to the Hershey Company, the town of Hershey, and the people who built it and lived there.

www.thehersheycompany.com
Official website of the company that Milton Hershey
founded; includes a timeline and news about the company's
history, along with details of its many current brand names.

www.hersheypark.com
Find out more about the amusement park near the
chocolate factory. Videos show you what it looks like to go
on the scariest rides!